Th

Z

This edition published in 2003

10 9 8 7 6 5 4 3 2 1

A CIP catalogue record for this book is available
from the British Library

ISBN 1 84222 813 3

Project editor: Martin Corteel
Project art direction: Darren Jordan
Production: Lisa French

Printed in Singapore

The Little Book of David Beckham

UNOFFICIAL & UNAUTHORISED

COMPILED AND EDITED BY ROB WIGHTMAN

CARLTON
BOOKS

Introduction

David Beckham is not the best footballer on the planet, fine player though he undoubtedly is. The London-born sarong-wearing England captain is, however, the game's most recognisable icon. His sporting career has been a roller-coaster ride of delicious curling free-kicks, gut-busting match-winning performances, an infamous sending-off and perhaps the most high-profile transfer in football history. Throughout, his ability to triumph over adversity on the field and catch the eye off it have won him friends (and enemies), fame and a vast fortune.

Beckham's extravagant lifestyle, charismatic personality and rich sporting ability have attracted a wealth of witty, stinging and perceptive comments, some favourable, others less so. This collection of soundbites represents just a fraction of what has been said and written about a naturally shy man whose knack of attracting global attention is virtually unrivalled.

‘ All I ever wanted to do was kick a football about. It didn't enter my head to do anything else. ’

David Beckham

'When the Manchester United talent scout finally came knocking on the door, and when he signed a contract on his 14th birthday, it is fair to say that the last thing this modest young man felt was surprise.'

Writer and journalist **Julie Burchill**

‘ Without a structure, a club, the team, the right set-up, neither Roy Keane, David Beckham, Eric Cantona nor any other 'star' would shine as brightly, if at all. ’

Roy Keane *insists that Manchester United is bigger than any individual*

❝ When you are a great player,
you can play for any team
in the world. ❞

Wily old sage **Paolo di Canio**
discusses Beckham's qualities in March 2000

❛I love being a professional footballer. From the moment I first kicked a ball I never wanted to be anything else.❜

David Beckham

‘ Beckham has great vision and we must put a man on him all the time to stop him getting in those dangerous crosses. ’

Franz Beckenbauer *tells Germany how to cope with Beckham at Euro 2000. England beat Germany 1–0 with Alan Shearer scoring from a Beckham cross.*

‘ I am sure he is very well known. But if you want me to discuss his technical qualities, I don't know... I'm at a risk of saying something really stupid here because I genuinely don't have the slightest idea. I don't follow football. ’

Argentina striker **Gabriel Batistuta**
struggles to talk about Beckham

❛In the modern game, where money talks, usually in a foreign language, the kind of loyalty and commitment that the six lads personify is a precious commodity.❜

Roy Keane *praises Manchester United's home-grown stars, Beckham among them*

❛Glory, believing the publicity, has cost us. Rolex watches, garages full of cars, ******* mansions, set up for life, forgot about the game, lost the hunger that got you the Rolex, the cars, the mansion.❜

Roy Keane *lets rip at United team-mates becoming sloppy after the club's Champions League exit in April 2002. It is not known whether Beckham is one of those he meant to criticise.*

‘Without any doubt much of the success of United is down to Alex Ferguson. My relationship with him has always been one of great respect. ’

David Beckham

❛ Never, never, never. Nobody at Real has ever spoken about Beckham and I don't want to start now. We are very happy with our current team and will never, ever sign Beckham. ❜

Real Madrid president **Florentino Pérez**,
April 30, 2003

'No one knows what'll happen in the future but I am convinced my son doesn't want to leave Manchester United and it would break his heart if he did go and that might be when he retires.'

Ted Beckham, *David's father, plays down rumours that his son will move to Madrid, April 2003*

‘ At the time the goal went in my Dad was so excited that he jumped up and head-butted the guy in the row in front of him. I think Mum just cried her eyes out. She couldn't stop telling the people around her that I was her son. **’**

David Beckham, *describes his debut goal for United*

‘ My dad has always drummed it into me to be polite, to say hello, to speak to people, because ultimately they are the ones who pay your wages. ’

David Beckham

❛I'd rather jack it in
than leave United. They're the only
team I've ever wanted to play for.
I'm absolutely gutted over
what's happened.❜

David Beckham *comments*
on Manchester United's plans to sell him
to Barcelona, June 2003

'Madrid have engaged Beckham because he's one of the best English footballers of all times whose spirit of adventure, dedication and comradeship has always been acknowledged.'

Florentino Pérez, *2 July 2003*

‘ Beckham is a central midfielder in exile on the wing. Whatever he is like as a person, his standard on the pitch is so high, he is so competitively brave and his touch so clean that, as the ball flies through the air, fans can read the make of it. ’

Real Madrid *sporting director Jorge Valdano, June 2003*

' Goalscoring has always been a buzz for me, whether it's been for my local Sunday side, or United. I try to keep a sense of fun about things, but it's a business as well and it's important for me to score and feel I'm contributing to the team. **'**

David Beckham

‘ Joining Real Madrid
is a dream come true. **'**

David Beckham
is pleased to sign for Madrid on 2 July 2003

‘ What they did after selling me
proved it was not a mistake,
but I'm not so sure about Beckham.
He's vital to United and I think they
have taken a huge gamble
by getting rid of him. ’

Paul Ince

❝ Fame is gauged on what you do on the pitch. Beckham scored a penalty [against Argentina] that shouldn't have been and England went out in the quarter-finals. That's no reason to go out and buy a Beckham shirt. ❞

Diego Maradona *after World Cup 2002*

❛ Myself and David Beckham...
it's like we're not actually human,
we're not allowed to have
trouble in our lives. ❜

Ronaldo

‘ When you see how Alex Ferguson has protected people like David Beckham and Ryan Giggs, you have to say that they are more aware of the problems of fame these days. ’

George Best *appreciates the way United look after their players nowadays*

' The showbiz element in his life, made inevitable by the pop-star status of his wife, Victoria, has sometimes caused me to worry about a possible threat to his chances of giving maximum expression to his huge talent. '

Sir Alex Ferguson *is concerned about Becks*

' I have never been a big drinker. I wasn't an angel but the only real tellings off I got were for stuff on the field. **"**

David Beckham

‘ The thought often crosses my mind that if I suggested to Becks or Laurent Blanc that we go to Mulligans for a 'session' they'd think that I'd gone mad! ’

Roy Keane *admits Beckham is one United team-mate who avoids lads' nights-out*

❛That's the girl for me and I'm going to get her.❜

David Beckham *tells best friend Gary Neville that Victoria is the girl of his dreams after seeing her in a Spice Girls video*

❛You do know, don't you, Victoria, that your dad will go mad.❜

Jackie Adams, *Victoria's mother, with her reaction to the news that her daughter is seeing David Beckham*

' There's always talk about how Victoria is in control and bosses me about, but we both wear the trousers in our relationship. '

David Beckham

' All I can remember about the whole thing is that my glasses were so steamed up I didn't actually see any of *Jerry Maguire* that night. **'**

Victoria Beckham *describes the first time she went to the cinema with David*

' It is not everyone who is able to enjoy what he always dreamed of doing, and then find his dream woman who says 'Yes' when he proposes to her. I guess I'm a pretty lucky young man. '

David Beckham

' He likes to borrow my knickers. **'**

Victoria Beckham *lets slip David's taste in underwear to TV presenter Johnny Vaughan*

' 'So,' says my dad, 'you're a footballer. **'**

Victoria Beckham *recounts David's first meeting with her parents*

' My first car was an Escort, then I bought myself a brand new Volkswagen Golf, then I had a Honda Prelude which was a club car; my fourth car was an M3 Convertible and my fifth is the Porsche. I like changing cars, and I suppose if I can afford to do it, I'll keep doing it. It isn't a crime to have a nice car. '

David Beckham

‘To me, merchandising is an extra and derives from the fact that I am a footballer. It doesn't interfere with the football part of my life, which is the most important. People love me because of football.’

David Beckham

‘ No celebrity has ever seemed so untouched by money as Beckham does, yet so infinitely commercial. ’

Julie Burchill

❝I wish I had scored that goal or one like it. It was one of those goals every player would like to score.❞

Eric Cantona *admires Beckham's halfway-line goal at Wimbledon, August 1996*

‘ What Eric [Cantona] stood for was perfection. If Eric had a go at you, it wasn't because he deliberately wanted to be nasty, it was to show you that you shouldn't be content with second best. ’

David Beckham

‘ I could not believe that anybody could ever accuse him of not being focused. Coming from Hoddle, who was one of England's most skilful footballers, it was truly amazing. In fact, I thought it was an insult. ’

Former Manchester United youth coach **Eric Harrison**, *who coached Beckham during his formative years*

❜It was the World Cup.
I had been thinking about that
since I was a kid.**❜**

David Beckham *reacts to Glenn Hoddle's*
accusation that he wasn't focused
at the 1998 World Cup

‘I was determined to stress that David shouldn't be made a scapegoat for what happened. ’

Glenn Hoddle *tries to protect Beckham after his World Cup sending-off*

‘ If he hadn't got sent off we would have had 11 men on the pitch and would have won the game. ’

Glenn Hoddle *makes Beckham a scapegoat for England's exit from the 1998 World Cup*

❛I think everyone should be allowed to do what they want to do without people making an issue out of colour. I feel very strongly about that.❜

David Beckham *expresses his loathing of racism*

‘ They are cheerleaders and ambassadors for heterosexuality, as Charles and Diana, Andrew and Fergie and Edward and Sophie were intended to be. ’

Julie Burchill *describes David and Victoria's relationship*

' People think that footballers are macho homophobic beer drinkers, but it doesn't bother me one bit whether someone's gay or straight. '

David Beckham

' It is an interesting paradox that these high priests of heterosexuality are then the campest act since Liberace. '

Julie Burchill

'It was a nasty, catty, underhand gesture and must have snapped the serene self-control which had stayed strong through so many years of jibes and jeering from his own countrymen, who had always seemed more offended by a football player who uses conditioner than by a football player who regularly hit his wife.'

Julie Burchill *describes Beckham's World Cup red card*

' Simeone, who's supposed to be
a tough-tackling midfielder,
went down like a sack of spuds. '

Phil Neville

❛I thought it would be wise to make a gesture which would close the whole issue on the World Cup, so I shook hands and swapped shirts with Simeone.**❜**

David Beckham *on playing against Diego Simeone in the Champions League, March 1999*

‘ None of us blamed him.
It's silly to blame one player.
We win, lose or draw as a team,
no matter what one player does. ’

Gary Neville *sticks up for Beckham after his red card*
against Argentina

❛Growing up, Bryan Robson was my hero and I wanted to wear the number seven just like him.❜

David Beckham

'A really fine player in every respect
and he has two feet
which a lot of people say
players don't have these days.'

Jimmy Hill *assesses Beckham's ability*

‘To follow those two was incredible. I was absolutely delighted, but also nervous. I knew I'd have to play well to keep it. Both players had such an influence on me.**’**

David Beckham *on being allowed to wear the famous number seven shirt, also worn at Manchester United by Bryan Robson and Eric Cantona*

'His Adidas boot might be good,
but he could do it with Dr Martens on.
It's an art form.'

Chris Waddle *on Beckham's ability
from free-kicks*

❝ To play alongside him was
simply an honour. **❞**

David Beckham *expresses his delight at playing in
the same team as United legend Eric Cantona*

' I think I'd have moved
to Outer Mongolia. **'**

Paul Merson *doesn't think he would have coped with the vitriol
Beckham received after the 1998 World Cup*

‘ Beckham thrills me.
He possesses terrific skills. ’

Dutch legend **Johan Cruyff**
*after Manchester United knock Internazionale out of the
Champions League in March 1999*

‘I wasn't going to leave Man United. The way the fans were to me and the way the manager was to me made me even more determined to stay. ’

David Beckham *on newspaper speculation he would be driven abroad after his sending-off against Argentina*

❛You know the hype has gone too far when you seek a picture of David with a noose around his neck in a leading tabloid newspaper. That's frightening.❜

Glenn Hoddle

‘ Counselling of some sort would help, perhaps from Eileen Drewery. ’

England manager **Glenn Hoddle** *suggests ways to help Beckham handle criticism*

‘ Ten heroic lions and one stupid boy. ’

Daily Mirror *headline after Beckham's World Cup sending-off*

‘Fatherhood made a man
of Beckham.’

Daily Mirror headline *after England skipper*
Beckham scores crucial winning goal against Finland three years later

' Ever since his formative years, he has practised from morning until night... You won't find anybody more dedicated than David. **'**

Former Manchester United youth coach **Eric Harrison** *applauds Beckham's commitment*

‘ David Beckham is Britain's finest striker of a football not because of God-given talent but because he practises with a relentless application that the vast majority of gifted players wouldn't contemplate. ’

Sir Alex Ferguson

‘ He's not big-headed
and couldn't afford to be
in a dressing-room like ours. ’

Jaap Stam *admires Beckham's modesty.*
Both players have since been sold by Manchester United

‘ We don't expect our intellectuals to be great footballers, but for some reason we expect our great footballers to be intellectuals. ’

Julie Burchill

❝ I'd play anywhere for United... although I'm not too sure how Peter Schmeichel would react if I put gloves on. **❞**

A very young **David Beckham**

❛I'll admit that David will not be asked to take a turn in the black chair of *Mastermind*, but I doubt whether I'd be wanted in there either.❜

Jaap Stam *makes the stunning revelation that he and David Beckham are not the cleverest people to have kicked a football*

❛ When the chips are down on the football field, you can bet your life that David Beckham won't be found wanting. **❜**

Sir Alex Ferguson

' David is not thick, he's just a normal guy having to put up with a lot of shit thrown at him by people don't even know his true personality. **'**

Jaap Stam *defends his team-mate*

❛ David is one of those people who can wake up in the morning and he looks great, with stubble, without stubble. He never has spots, he never has a bad hair day. But I'm very insecure about the way I look. ❜

Victoria Beckham

❛ I don't know if you can find anyone better in the world today. He is very important to us. **❜**

Sven Goran Eriksson *praises Beckham*

‘ When players don't respect a
manager then it's no good any
more, but he's a great manager,
and we all stick by him. ’

David Beckham *defends England manager*
Sven Goran Eriksson

‘Every time he passes the ball, there is a thought behind where it is going. There is thought behind everything David does.’

Sven Goran Eriksson *keeps praising Beckham*

❝ She's in pop and David's got another image. He's developed this 'fashion thing'. I saw his transition to a different person. ❞

Sir Alex Ferguson *reveals misgivings about David Beckham's lifestyle, July 2003*

'It is a massive challenge for me and all I can really do is try to disturb him and kick him as much as possible.'

*Liechtenstein's enforcer **Fredi Gigon***
on taking on David Beckham in the Euro 2004 qualifiers

‘ When I got my last chance, Teddy Sheringham said he would have it but I decided I'd take it. ’

David Beckham *pulls rank on his team-mate to score the injury-time free-kick that takes England to the 2002 World Cup*

‘ I want Beckham's shirt, too.
He is a god, not a footballer. ’

Liechtenstein goalkeeper **Peter Jehle**

'It is fun, if only briefly,
to try to imagine how the
Beckhams' brains work.**'**

Julie Burchill

❝ The event seemed to capture the spirit of Posh and Becks as individuals, a couple and a culture; a curious combination of childlike narcissism, conspicuous consumption and Disneyesque innocence. ❞

Biographer **Andrew Morton** *gives his opinion of the Beckhams' wedding*

❛Nothing compares to what I've got with Victoria and that's why I married her. I see us as the perfect couple.❜

David Beckham

‘ That the Beckhams take such an obvious physical delight in each other must be very galling indeed for the balding, softening fortysomething male journalist whose sex life started to slide years ago. ’

Writer and journalist **Julie Burchill**

❛Billed as the wedding of the year, the sense of illusion and self delusion was encapsulated in the fact a couple, who publicly professed such intense love for each other, turned what is traditionally seen as a spiritual union into a photographic shoot.❜

Writer **Andrew Morton** *expresses his distaste at the Beckham wedding*

❛ He makes the clamour and loutishness of modern celebrity recede, gliding untouched through a scum-tossed sea of thongs, sarongs and unsolicited Adolf Eichmann T-shirts. ❜

Writer and journalist **Julie Burchill**

'As long as he is a good captain and a good player I'm very happy. It's up to him how he cuts his hair. '

Sven Goran Eriksson *extinguishes the furore surrounding Beckham's Mohawk hairstyle*

'The most important thing to me
is my family, but without my football
I'm a lost man.'

David Beckham *bemoans the injury
that almost saw him miss the 2002 World Cup*

❛I have no doubt that Euro 2004 is something that is well within our grasp: that this our spirit is unshakeable, our belief in each other is rock solid.❜

David Beckham *is optimistic about England long-term prospects*

❝ It has impressed me how he has taken on the role as captain for England I did not see him as a captain because he is a quiet lad. **❞**

Sir Alex Ferguson *discusses Beckham's role as England skipper*

‘As I was trying to stand up that was when he kicked me from behind. And I took advantage of that.**’**

Diego Simeone *admits cheating to get Beckham sent off*

‘ Please, don't take any penalties. ’

Victoria Beckham's request to David before the
2002 World Cup finals

'As soon as I hit the ball, my mind went blank. It was the release of everything that has gone on.**'**

David Beckham *relives his penalty against Argentina at the 2002 World Cup*

' It's important for me to do normal
things like go to the supermarket,
even if people are surprised to see me
buying fruit. To do normal things
helps me with my mental balance.
I don't want a chauffeur here.
I want to drive myself around. '

David Beckham *looks forward to life in Spain*

' People always talk about the manager and myself having our ups and downs, and of course we've had our share, but that's just part and parcel of life and we have always had a good relationship. '

David Beckham *talks about Fergie after signing for Real Madrid*

' Fergie has not spoken to David for months now. To do all this behind David's back is awful. '

Ted Beckham *reacts to Manchester United's agreement to sell David to Barcelona, June 2003*

'He's the reason why I joined Manchester United in the first place, apart from obviously being the club I supported. He is the reason why I am the player I am today and he would never have put me in the team at 17 if he hadn't had a good feeling about me.'

David Beckham *on Sir Alex Ferguson, 3 July 2003*

'The way I see it, there are at least 20 players in the world who are better in his position. He fits in very well in the Manchester United system and is a quality player in dead ball situations, but playing in Spain is a different thing.'

Defender **Patrick Andersson** *didn't want Beckham at Barcelona anyway*

' Nobody should ever underestimate David Beckham. At times I have disagreed with decisions he has taken off the field but he has a stubbornness that can't be broken and he will make up his own mind, whatever Alex Ferguson may think. **'**

Sir Alex Ferguson

' When he went pale and then started being sick in the early hours, there was no way I was going to leave him. '

David Beckham *explains why he stayed at home with baby Brooklyn instead of attending training in February 2000*

‘I don't think anything will ever match that Treble season of 1998–99. I will spend the rest of my career trying to equal it.**’**

David Beckham

❛ David Beckham is the only British player who would get into the Brazilian squad. ❜

Brazilian superstar **Rivaldo**

❛I've never been a good loser.
Like every other player in the team,
I hate it. ❜

David Beckham

' His body language, scowling, frowning but resolutely silent, made clear that much more than his eye had been wounded. **'**

Andrew Morton *describes the aftermath of the incident when Sir Alex Ferguson kicked a boot in Beckham's face*

❛If I tried 100 times or a million times it could not happen again. If it could I would have carried on playing. ❜

Sir Alex Ferguson *gives his own account of the Flying Boot incident*

‘ The division between Ferguson
and Beckham represented the
struggle between Old Man and
New Man, the traditional macho
soccer culture versus the changing
model of masculinity, the modern
gentle man. ’

Andrew Morton *analyses the conflict
personalities between Beckham and Ferguson*

' There are only a certain amount
of people you meet in your life who
leave a real impression on you,
and Alex Ferguson is certainly one
of those people. Next to my
Dad, he's been the biggest
influence on me … '

David Beckham

❝ The real opportunity only came a week before we announced the signing. It was the fastest signing I have made. We were presented with an offer, the player was in agreement and it was all done in a matter of hours. ❞

Florentino Pérez

' What happens if it's 0–0 with a minute to go and they get a free-kick? If Beckham was there you would back him to score. Now they won't have that luxury. '

Paul Ince *thinks United may have made a mistake selling Beckham to Madrid*

❛If I had to pick a weakness in Beckham's game it's his left foot. But that's like saying Maradona's right foot wasn't too clever.❜

George Best

‘She turned to him and said, 'Well, Michael Jordan hasn't done too badly with the No. 23 …' and that was the moment that we reached a joint decision. I turned to David and said '23 it is'.’

Jorge Valdano

‘ Barcelona, AC Milan and Inter Milan were the other clubs but Real Madrid was the one that really interested me and the only one I got excited about. ’

David Beckham *reveals the options open to him when leaving Old Trafford, 3 July 2003*

‘ We were stuck in the middle of this discussion about whether the No. 4 or the No. 23 was the one he should choose... we couldn't reach a conclusion until his wife intervened. ’

Real Madrid sporting director **Jorge Valdano** *hints at the balance of power in the Beckham household*

❛ David Beckham and I were standing in the centre-circle when the crowd started calling me names. I said to him: 'I suppose you're used all this.' He grinned and replied: 'Yeah, but in my case, it's not true!' ❜

Referee **Graham Poll**

❛He [Beckham] cannot kick with his left foot, he cannot head a ball, he cannot tackle and he doesn't score many goals.
Apart from that he's all right.**❜**

George Best's *(probably tongue-in-cheek)*
verdict on Beckham

❝ No one is ever allowed to get too big-time at United. At Old Trafford, you have to remember that all the big players leave and the club goes on. ❞

David Beckham

‘ David has really proved that he is one of the best players in the world. **’**

Eric Cantona

‘ I'd like to be known as a good bloke, someone who never let anybody down, who behaved properly, who did right by people, who treated other people the way he liked to be treated himself. ’

David Beckham

❛A player can only be considered truly world class if he has played for Real Madrid in his career.❜

Brazilian defender **Roberto Carlos**

'There have been so many
United greats who wore it.
I hope I did it justice.'

David Beckham
on wearing the United number seven shirt

❛I thought Beckham would be a keen golfer. Most English footballers seem to play the game. I'd certainly like to take him out on the golf course and show him what a great game it is.❜

Golfer **Sergio Garcia** *looks forward to Beckham's arrival in Spain*

'The club will always have a special place in my heart. I have always been a Manchester United supporter and will always follow them.'

David Beckham *says goodbye to United fans as he decamps to Madrid*

❛A player of Beckham's quality makes any team shine. An individual like Beckham, with the presence so great beyond the world sport, with such international resonance, reinforces our club's objective, which is to project Real Madrid as a universal phenomenon.❜

Real Madrid president **Florentino Pérez**

‘ I don't care about Beckham. I've admired Victoria ever since she was a Spice Girl. And I'm not moving from here until I see her. ’

A teenage Spanish girl tells **Hello!** *magazine which of the Beckhams she wants to welcome to Madrid*

‘ He's as fit as a bull. ’

Real Madrid doctor **Alfonso Del Corral** *gives Beckham the all-clear to sign for the Spanish giants, July 2003*

‘ Our problems form part of the past and they are now forgotten. I'm looking forward to coming up against him again and now that he has joined Madrid I will get the chance. ’

Deportivo La Coruña hard man **Aldo Duscher**, *who famously broke Beckham's metatarsal, welcomes the England skipper to Spain*

❛Real sent a shirt through the post. I have been wearing it around the house. Everywhere I go, I always bring back a kit for Brooklyn. He already had a Real kit but now he will be able to wear it outside the house!❜

David Beckham

❛ There's more to his importance than on the pitch though. He is a true hero with the fans and his commercial value to United was huge. I'm sure the players there are surprised he's gone just like I am. **❜**

Paul Ince *questions the wisdom of selling Beckham to Madrid*

'I know David Beckham had a problem fighting off autograph hunters when he went to his favourite restaurant. He's now reverted to take-aways, but luckily I have not had similar problems.'

Jaap Stam *is relieved not to have Beckham's high profile*

❛ Even on the Sunday morning of Princess Diana's death, I had photographers and journalists outside my house, which I thought was disgraceful. ❜

David Beckham

‘ When he wants you to kick the ball he yells 'It it', which sounds really funny. Then when you get into the back of his car, he says 'Don't scuff me levver!' We're always imitating him, but he doesn't mind, he just laughs. ’

Ryan Giggs *is amused by Beckham's accent*

❛I spoke to Louise Nurding for only ten minutes in a club and it was in the papers the next day that we were a couple.❜

David Beckham *on tabloid tittle-tattle, December 1996*

‘ I was very angry with his tackle on Tomislav Kocijan. That's why I had a go at him and said I did not like his wife's music. ’

Sturm Graz midfielder **Roman Mahlich** *describes a spat with Beckham*

'I have a camera up my backside
almost 24 hours a day.'

David Beckham
(You wonder how he plays football with such a predicament!)

‘ David's ability is unquestionable and so is his work rate – he covers miles of ground for a midfielder. His crossing is immaculate, as are his free-kicks. ’

George Best, *July 2003*

' Beckham didn't deserve
to be elected best player in the
world. When he can do
something else apart from cross
perhaps he will. ,

George Best's *opinion of Beckham being voted
second best player in the world, January 2000*

Newspapers and magazines

The Daily Telegraph
Daily Mirror
FourFourTwo magazine
The Guardian
Hello! magazine
Marca
Manchester Evening News
News of the World
The Observer Sport Monthly
Sports Illustrated
The Sun
UNITED The Official Manchester United Magazine

Sources
Books

Beckham My Story, David Beckham, Manchester United Books
(an imprint of Andre Deutsch Ltd), 1998.

Beckham My World, David Beckham, Hodder & Stoughton, 2000.

Blessed: The autobiography, George Best, Ebury Press, 2001.

Burchill on Beckham, Yellow Jersey Press, 2002.

For Club and Country, Gary and Phil Neville with Sam Pilger and
Justyn Barnes, Manchester United Books, 1998.

Head to Head, Jaap Stam with Jeremy Butler, CollinsWillow
(an imprint of HarperCollins Publishers), 2001.

Keane: The autobiography, Roy Keane with Eamon Dunphy, Michael
Joseph (an imprint of Penguin Books), 2002.

Learning to Fly: The autobiography, Victoria Beckham,
Penguin Books, 2001.

Managing My Life, Sir Alex Ferguson, Hodder & Stoughton, 1999.

My 1998 World Cup Story, Glenn Hoddle, Andre Deutsch Ltd, 1998.

Posh and Becks, Andrew Morton, Michael O'Mara Books Ltd, 2000.

United Heroes, Rebecca Tow & Simon Davies,
Manchester United Books, 2003.

The View From The Dugout, Eric Harrison, The Parrs Wood Press, 2001.

ROB WIGHTMAN has followed the career of David Beckham ever since the midfielder scored on his Manchester United European debut against Galatasaray in December 1994. While Beckham has gone from boy next door to the planet's most recognised football icon, Rob has carved out a career as a football writer and journalist. A biographer of Manchester United's previous number seven, Eric Cantona, Rob is a regular contributor to the *Manchester United official magazine*, *FourFourTwo*, *Shoot Monthly* and several national newspapers.

Television and radio

BBC1
Big Breakfast, Channel 4
MUTV

Internet sites

BBC.co.uk
Man Utd.com
www.saidwhat.co.uk